Baby Animals in the Wild!

Giraffe Calves in the Wild

by Marie Brandle

Bullfrog Books

Ideas for Parents and Teachers

Bullfrog Books let children practice reading informational text at the earliest reading levels. Repetition, familiar words, and photo labels support early readers.

Before Reading

- Discuss the cover photo. What does it tell them?

- Look at the picture glossary together. Read and discuss the words.

Read the Book

- "Walk" through the book and look at the photos. Let the child ask questions. Point out the photo labels.

- Read the book to the child, or have him or her read independently.

After Reading

- Prompt the child to think more. Ask: Giraffe calves eat leaves that grow in tall trees. How do they do this?

Bullfrog Books are published by Jump!
5357 Penn Avenue South
Minneapolis, MN 55419
www.jumplibrary.com

Library of Congress Cataloging-in-Publication Data

Names: Brandle, Marie, 1989– author.
Title: Giraffe calves in the wild / by Marie Brandle.
Description: Minneapolis, MN: Jump!, Inc., [2023]
Series: Baby animals in the wild!
Includes index. | Audience: Ages 5–8
Identifiers: LCCN 2022010058 (print)
LCCN 2022010059 (ebook)
ISBN 9798885240659 (hardcover)
ISBN 9798885240666 (paperback)
ISBN 9798885240673 (ebook)
Subjects: LCSH: Giraffe—Infancy—Juvenile literature.
Classification: LCC QL737.U56 B73 2023 (print)
LCC QL737.U56 (ebook)
DDC 599.638—dc23/eng/20220314
LC record available at https://lccn.loc.gov/2022010058
LC ebook record available at https://lccn.loc.gov/2022010059

Editor: Eliza Leahy
Designer: Molly Ballanger

Photo Credits: Merrillie Redden/Shutterstock, cover; Jamie Stamey/iStock, 1; gracious_tiger/Shutterstock, 3; Tony Crocetta/Biosphoto/SuperStock, 4; Sergio Pitamitz/Alamy, 5, 23tm; camacho9999/iStock, 6–7; Nick Fox/Shutterstock, 8–9, 23tr; Suzi Eszterhas/Minden Pictures/SuperStock, 10–11; Pranesh Luckan/Shutterstock, 12, 23bm; laytonjeff/iStock, 13; Artushfoto/Dreamstime, 14–15, 23tl; Eric Isselee/Shutterstock, 16; Chedko/Shutterstock, 16–17, 23bl; Judith Andrews/Shutterstock, 18; MyImages - Micha/Shutterstock, 19; castigatio/iStock, 20–21; pandapaw/Shutterstock, 22; Maciej Czekajewski/Shutterstock, 23br; Svetlana Foote/Shutterstock, 24.

Printed in the United States of America at Corporate Graphics in North Mankato, Minnesota.

Table of Contents

Growing Tall

A giraffe calf is born.
It stands right away.

The calf is a baby.

But it is already six feet (1.8 meters) tall!

It stays by Mom.
It drinks her milk.

tongue

Mom grooms the calf.
She licks its fur.

The calf runs!
Its long legs help.

mane

The calf has a mane.

spot

The calf has spots, too.

Giraffes live on the savanna.
Spots help them blend in.

Lions hunt giraffes.
Giraffes live in herds.
This keeps them safe.

lion

herd

The calf grows taller.

Its neck is long.

It reaches leaves.

It eats.

It grows up!

Parts of a Giraffe Calf

What are the parts of a giraffe calf? Take a look!

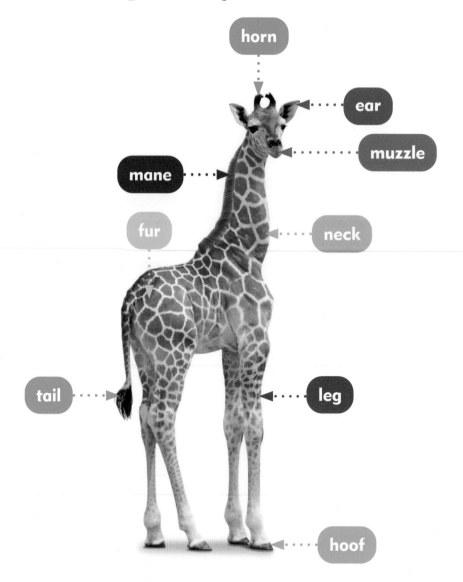

horn

ear

muzzle

mane

fur

neck

tail

leg

hoof

Picture Glossary

blend in
To look like things nearby.

calf
A young giraffe.

grooms
Cleans.

herds
Groups of animals that stay or move together.

mane
The thick hair on the head and neck of some animals.

savanna
A flat, grassy plain with few or no trees.

Index

To Learn More

Finding more information is as easy as 1, 2, 3.

❶ Go to www.factsurfer.com

❷ Enter "giraffecalves" into the search box.

❸ Choose your book to see a list of websites.